TEACHING SCHOOL ON THE WYOMING PRAIRIE IN THE 1940's

TEACHING SCHOOL ON THE WYOMING PRAIRIE IN THE 1940's

A Memoir

A Historical True Story

By EDNA OGLE

ISBN 978-1-938859-40-3

Printed in the United States of America

by Tattered Cover Press

Book design by Abby Hoke, www.aebgraphics.com

Watercolor cover designed and created by Nancy Maher

If you would like to contact the author,

Edna's e-mail address is ednaogle@comcast.net

Dedication

Dedicated to my father, Iver Nathaniel Youngren, whose hard work and perseverance sent me to college to be a teacher.

Acknowledgements

Many thanks to my creative writing teacher, Danielle Steinfeld, in Arvada, Colorado for encouragement, typing and editing my book. A very special thanks to my daughter, Marty Harris, whose hours of typing and revising made this book possible, for it could not have been published without her continual encouragement and inspiration.

Thank you Dee Miller, for starting me on the path by introducing me to the author, Terry Burns, whose information was invaluable.

I am also grateful to my daughter Ruth, and her husband Ray for continued support, and my sister Sigrid for her encouraging phone calls.

My "cheering section" at the Creative Writing class for two years, meant so very much. Thank you each one for your stimulating suggestions.

A very special thanks to Nancy Maher, who created the appealing watercolor cover.

Thank you everyone!

Prologue

I am in my eighties. Another good friend has just passed away—leaving a 100-year-old house to be cleaned out. After the service, the family slowly and reluctantly said good-by, and returned to their homes and their daily routines. One son, Tom, was left to enter the home, quietly and alone, to begin sorting through 60 years of memories.

Having no romantic attic, I knew what I must do…sort and throw away! I went out to the garage to begin clearing out. My children and grandchildren have very busy, continuing lives. What would a 1940 diploma or a crushed corsage from a special date mean to them?!

I began with my Dad's suitcase. The lid fell back revealing a tattered, old, manila yearbook. It was from my first teaching assignment in the 1940's. A flood of memories splashed over me as I remembered the excitement and anticipation of living alone in the school house, teaching all eight grades while the unending wind swept across the prairie. I read the title, "Ulm Longhorns," and then my arms hugged it to my chest. Yes, here was the book that told the story, with a love story hidden between the pages. Yes, it is time!

Part I

Ulm

1
Graduation

It was 1945. Graduation was over. I would miss the small Lutheran campus in Wahoo, Nebraska, with chapel every day, girls' and boys' dorms, Old Main, the friendly dining hall (where we could come to breakfast in our PJs under our trench coats), singing the Messiah all together at Christmas, the Music Hall and all the college fun.

Reluctant to go back home to Sheridan, Wyoming, we girls decided to stay in the dorm for the summer and work the night shift at the defense factory close by. We wanted to help the troops and be a part of the war effort, or perhaps we just wanted to be on our own.

My job was to drive the tractor outside to the boxcars to load the empty bombs and carry them inside to be filled with the explosive powder. The former driver had dozed off and pushed the wrong lever, causing the crane to fall back and crush her. She died instantly and I was scared! That was the time in my life that I began to be a heavy coffee drinker, for the nights were very long. Because of the danger involved, my paycheck was larger than the paychecks of the girls who worked on the assembly line, but my coffee bill was more than theirs, especially since I was on the graveyard shift.

But now the summer was over. My father informed me in no uncertain terms, in an expensive three-minute telephone call, that I needed a job soon and that it was time for me to come home.

As the train began to slow down, I found myself getting very anxious. Now what? Where do I start? A full-time teaching job? My two-year college diploma, packed proudly in my suitcase, stated that I was "qualified" to teach Elementary Education. Where? Uncertainty flooded my brain.

I realized that my fun, secure college life was over. I would be back home, living with my parents in Sheridan in August, with no sign of a teaching job.

The train squeaked to a stop. There were my parents, awaiting the inevitable. Dad took care of my suitcases; Mama hugged me and said softly, "There was an ad in the paper today."

Driving home, Dad began his monologue on the garden, the renters, the relatives, etc. He spoke loudly, as he had a hearing loss, thus Mom and I couldn't get a word in edgewise. When we arrived home, he went out to feed the chickens. Mama and I sat down with the newspaper.

Wanted: School teacher for grades

one to eight. Teacherage furnished.

$100 a month. Call Hedwik Miech

278-1828.

"But where is the school?" I asked, as I envisioned being shipped to Timbuktu. Just then Dad came in and took over.

"There's the phone. You might as well call right now." Armed with a tablet and pencil, I reached for the phone.

An eager voice replied hurriedly, the long distance rates on her mind: "Oh yes, Edna, your Aunt Lily told me you were coming home. You know, we taught together at Dutch Creek School. The school is in Ulm, a small town a few miles from Sheridan. You can take the train home on weekends. You live in the schoolhouse." She continued, "There are two separate rooms—no electricity or inside water, but two good coal stoves. I live just down the road by the post office."

She paused. "Tell your folks 'Hello.' I'll get the contract to you. Talk to you soon." The three-minute call was over.

Waves of emotion swept over me. I felt overwhelmed with disbelief, surprise, frustration—yes, even some excitement! I couldn't help but wonder if Aunt Lily (who loved to "manage" things), Hedwik, and perhaps even Mama, had been planning. I seemed to need managers in my life. Indecisiveness was my weakness. I had read in a magazine that being indecisive could be a mental problem. I tore out the page and threw it away!

I looked at Mama. She was smiling contently. Impulsively, I said, "I think I'll get on the bicycle and ride down to Custer School. I won't be gone long."

My favorite ride was down the dirt road to my first elementary school where, many years ago, I had walked with my mother on my first day of school. I sat on the broad steps as the playground swings swayed in the breeze. I pondered what was happening. I realized mother would like me close a while longer. She knew of my dreams to go to Africa or China someday. This year could just be a stepping stone.

Slowly, I got back on the bicycle and began to pedal. The gentle breeze began to blow—my spirits lifted—a school of my own, all grades and sizes, out on the prairie. I began to pedal faster as I told myself, "Let's go for it!"

In a few days, Mrs. Miech (Hedwik) came by the house, as she was in town to purchase quart jars for canning their corn and green beans.

"Oh, Edna," she greeted me, "We're all so relieved to get a teacher this year. There are fourteen students and all eight grades, so you'll be busy! Everyone is ready for school. It's been a really hot summer."

She paused to take a breath as she wiped the perspiration from her face and took the contract from her canvas bag. We settled ourselves at the dining room table, but she was not a person to "settle" for long. She was thirty-ish, slim, vibrant and exuberant. I liked her instantly.

"I really must be going, just sign here." She paused. "School begins the day after Labor Day, see you soon."

She was gone.

The days passed quickly as my emotions changed from exuberance to anxiety. Mom began sewing my "teacher" clothes: a practical cotton black skirt and three blouses, all made from the same pattern, with short puffed sleeves and a yoke. She "found" a piece of eyelet for the yoke on one of them, for a "special occasion," she said.

As she sewed, and as we thought about my first job, she told me of her first job in Washington, D.C., during World War I. She had wanted to be in Washington when her boyfriend, Harry Rush, came back from the war in France. He never came back. He was buried in France.

We had all heard her story many times, but I was glad to hear it again and thankful she had come back to Sheridan and married Iver Youngren, an immigrant from Sweden. Iver was so proud to marry a Swedish girl, for then all of his children would be 100% Swedish! For immigrants this was very important.

My dad called from the back porch, "If 'you people' (one of his favorite expressions) keep talking, we will never get to the train on time."

They took me to the depot. Dad helped me on the train as Mom said, "We'll see you on Friday, Sis." We waved as the train chugged out of town.

2
Arriving in Ulm

As the train click-clacked on the track, swaying gently, I gazed at the landscape as it changed from the town, to the country and then to the prairie, with its never-ending sagebrush and dirt roads. I dozed off.

Suddenly, with a screech of brakes, the train jerked to a stop.

"Miss," the conductor called, "this is Ulm."

I reached for my suitcase and the conductor helped me down the steep steps. I stepped back from the train as the engineer blew the shrill whistle and the train chugged away.

I just stood there, surveying the landscape—the quietness, the bleakness, no trees, only sagebrush—a gentle wind tossing it about. This was my new home, a new way of life—I was a teacher! It was an awesome moment.

I started down the well-worn path to the post office marked "Ulm, Wyo." The screen door hung loosely on the old frame building. Hesitantly, I pulled it open with the wooden handle on the left.

In the back of the store an elderly man was playing solitaire on a backless chair as the late afternoon sun shone through the dusty window. He wore a crumpled white shirt with elastic arm bands and wide gray suspenders. A top hat covered his curly hair as he sat enjoying his cigarette.

"Come on in, you must be the new school marm." He extended his hand. "Name is Jim McClelland."

"Glad to meet you, Jim. My name is Edna Youngren," I replied, shaking his warm, rough hand.

"You probably better get going," he continued. "It'll be dark before long. Hedwik is right across the street. She'll give you your kerosene lamps. By the way, do you play checkers?"

"Oh yes, I'd enjoy a game any time. See you later, Jim."

I closed the door and walked across the street toward the fenced white house with ivy covering the porch.

The screen door slammed open as a handsome collie jumped out, followed by a little blond boy and Hedwik.

"We've been expecting you, Edna," she smiled. "This is Donnie. He's four."

Donnie eagerly held up four fingers. A tall, blond, blue-eyed smiling boy appeared at his side.

"This is my Jim," she said proudly as she brushed his hair across his forehead with her hands. "He'll be in the eighth grade."

"Yes," Jim replied, "Rose, Norma, Nancy, Don and I will all be going in town for high school next year!"

The screen door slammed shut as a younger boy appeared. He sported dark, curly hair and a mischievous grin—a flannel shirt and jeans.

"My name is Bob," he said. "I'm in the fifth grade. Ike Corley, Edgar Ruski and I run around together and will help little Johnny in the first grade. He's kinda shy and scared about school, but we'll help," he repeated after he paused for breath.

"Thank you, Bob," I answered, thinking I would need all the help I could get!

"You boys get on with your chores and keep track of Donnie while I go up to the schoolhouse with Miss Youngren. Dad will be home soon."

Turning to me, she added, "Mike, my husband, is the section foreman here on the railroad. That's why we moved here. It's a lot of responsibility for him."

We began our walk up the road.

3
The Schoolhouse

We walked slowly up the dirt road to the schoolhouse.

There were no trees, just level plains stretching endlessly, as the soft wind blew the sagebrush across the road. The schoolhouse was plainly visible with a fresh coat of white paint, rows of sparkling windows and a wide porch with four inviting steps. The privy stood staunch and still, away from the schoolhouse.

We paused at the broken pump in the front yard and started up the steps. The sun was slowly closing the day as Hedwik opened the front door. We entered the hallway where the children would hang their wraps and deposit their lunch pails. Everything was spotlessly clean, thanks to Hedwik and the boys. She opened the classroom door. I said nothing...it was awesome.

Sunlight poured through the windows on the west, settling on the worn, polished desks facing the large potbellied stove. Hedwik showed me the damper on the stove pipe for regulating the air. I tried to act like I understood, never having built a fire in my life. She pointed to the coal pail and said the kindling was in the coal bin in the hall…. Little did I realize that the stove would be my abomination, giving me smoky days and cold, frosty mornings.

The large oak teacher's desk sat in the corner, displaying a pencil sharpener and the recess bell, waiting to perform its duty . . . one of my favorite times. The scent of the oiled pine floors, large storage cupboard and desks left a pleasant aroma. Erasers and chalk were on the blackboard shelf and the bulletin boards waited to be filled with the children's handiwork. The flag was in place with Washington and Lincoln hung on the wall. The tick-tock of the pendulum clock was like a friendly smile.

My youthful exuberance overcame my anxiety and I was anxious to get started. Leaving the schoolroom, we entered the teacherage. Gleaming clean windows, scrubbed table and chair, a two-burner kerosene stove, a single bed, freshly made, orange crate cupboards, colorful handmade throw rugs, a filled coal bucket by the polished stove, a well-worn desk and chair beneath the blackboard, where I read "Welcome, Miss Youngren"—all this greeted me as Hedwik put the kerosene lamp on the table.

Bob burst into the room with a quart jar of fresh milk and a basket. "Here's the churned butter, and the bread is still nice and warm," he announced as he put the basket on the table. He opened the window to put the milk on the outside sill. Jimmy followed him with two buckets of water. "These are for you, Miss Youngren, I'll put one in the hallway, with the dipper for all of us, and this one is yours. You can come down to our place after school and fill them, since the school pump doesn't work."

"Dad says the well is all dried up," added Bob.

"Mom, we'd better get back to the chores, and it's time to milk the cow," Jimmy said as he played with his yo-yo.

"Yes, we need to go. Just let me know if you need something."

"Thank you, Hedwik, for everything…the fresh bread smells so good."

"Oh, that's okay. Tomorrow will be an easy day, getting acquainted with the children. They'll leave early so you can start your lesson plans. The textbooks and curriculum are all in the school cupboard. You'll do fine," she added as she followed the boys. They left and ran down the road. As I wandered back into the classroom and sat at my desk, a frightening thought came to me…. Where do I start? What now?

I remembered doing my practice teaching at Story, Wyoming, staying at the ranch with Aunt Lily for three weeks. It was a small, white schoolhouse surrounded by swings, a teeter-totter, and a place to play kickball. The teacher loved children, and enjoyed teaching. The grade assignments were placed on the blackboard—reading, phonics, spelling and arithmetic were in the morning, geography and science in the afternoon—and all coming together for music, art and recess, which was a great time for getting acquainted with the individual children. Could I do as well?

I approached the large glassed-in bookcase, which stood like a challenging fortress. As I opened the door of the bookcase, there was the ultimate official book, *State of Wyoming, Curriculum for Rural Schools, Grades 1-8*. I had inherited from my father the wonderful gift of perennial optimism, but now I began to realize I needed to set aside my youthful exuberance for the seriousness of teaching all eight grades.... A first grader to introduce to reading (no *Sesame Street* TV in those days!), preparing five eighth graders for high school, with all the necessary skills, and all the grades in-between!

The room began darkening into evening. My shaking hand reached for the kerosene lamp on my desk. After lighting three matches, the light with its kerosene odor filled the room. The *Curriculum* read, "The textbooks are taken from the curriculum material. If a teacher effectively uses the books for the correct grade, the material will be covered." A wave or relief swept over me.

Just perhaps, after the first day getting acquainted, I could begin in earnest with plans for each individual child. I walked over to the blackboard, picked up the chalk and wrote, in my best Palmer Method handwriting,

Welcome to Ulm School

Today is September 8, 1945

My name is Miss Youngren

4
Beginnings

I awakened early, dressed in my new black skirt and "special occasion" blouse, and stepped out on the porch. The sun was warm and friendly; no need to start a fire in the forbidding stove that day.

Glancing at my watch, I went into the school room where the welcoming sun was streaming through the shiny, clean windows. The well-worn desks seemed beckoning, as if waiting for the children. I read over the list on my desk of plans for the day: introductions, distributing the textbooks, penmanship, lunch, reading aloud…getting acquainted.

They came, one group from up the road, and others in a pickup or truck. They began to play tag in the schoolyard, reluctant, and yet eager, to come in. At nine o'clock, I rang the bell and greeted them as they rushed in to claim their desks. The younger ones gathered in front, the middlers in the center, while the older students walked confidently to the back of the room to the larger desks.

I counted twelve...all spruced up for the first day of school. They looked up expectantly.

"I'm so glad you're all here this morning," I began. "My name is Miss Youngren," I said, pointing to the board.

An eager tow-headed boy spoke up, "Everybody isn't here. My sister Pauline is over at Nancy's helping with the threshers. Marie and I had to walk by ourselves today and that's a long walk!"

"Oh, thank you for telling me. I don't know about threshers."

"The crew comes with a combine every year to harvest the crops. Those men work hard and are really hungry," Rose volunteered from the back of the room.

"I'm glad they can help," I responded. "And I'm sure they'll be back soon. Now, I would like each of you, one at a time, to write your name and grade on the blackboard. Who would like to start?" They looked at each other, waiting.

Jimmy Miech stood. "I'll start."

Rose followed, then turned around and said, "May I write Pauline and Nancy's names? They'll probably be here tomorrow."

"Oh yes, thank you, Rose, then we'll have everyone." The little ones, Johnny, Marie and Mary Lou, participated and sat quietly. The three middle boys could not sit still…touching, laughing and teasing the girls, Yvonne and Arlene.

The eighth graders, Jimmy, Don, Rose and Norma, helped distribute the textbooks. Johnny Crackenburger was the only one in the first grade. He beamed as Jimmy gave him his books.

"Look, Jimmy, look at the horses in my book!"

Marie Ruski, combing her blonde curls with her fingers, thanked Don as he gave her the second-grade books. She poked Mary Lou and remarked, "Look at this brand new reading book!"

Mary Lou retorted, "It's not brand new. I read it last year. It was easy." She shrugged her shoulders.

Edgar, Bob and Ike took their books and shoved them in their desks then began putting their names on their new red Big Chief tablets from Jim's store.

They scrambled to sharpen their new pencils, cranking the pencil sharpener, which was fastened to my desk.

Yvonne and Arlene Pence were in the sixth grade and Pauline was a seventh grader. The eighth-grade books—geography, history, arithmetic, reading and English—were piled on their desks.

"We probably won't use these large geography books every day, Miss Youngren. Couldn't we keep them in the cupboard?"

"Good idea, Rose. And here are your bookmarks. Everyone needs one for each book, with your name on it. Then let's all stand and do some exercises!"

I asked Edgar Ruski to pass out the paper so they could practice their penmanship. Surprisingly, they responded like ducks to water. While the older ones practiced cursive, I worked with Johnny, our first grader, and Betty Lou, our second grader, on printing. Very quickly, Betty Lou informed me that she could do cursive! She did very well! They all became very proficient and aware of good writing during the year.

The morning passed quickly and all too soon it was time for lunch. Jimmy and Bob walked home as all of us went outside on the newly painted porch and sat on the steps. The three Pence girls, Norma, Yvonne and Mary Lou, shared their lunch of fried chicken from last night's supper. Don ate quietly on a lower step. Ike grabbed his sandwich from his sister Rose and sat out by the broken pump with Edgar, awaiting Bob's return. Johnny inched close to Don as they ate their lunch together.

It was a short break. We passed around the water bucket with the blue dipper. Marie wanted to ring the bell. It was a hot September day. They came inside and laid their heads on their desks while I read aloud from *The Secret Garden*. Reading aloud after lunch was to become a comfortable, restful routine.

We dismissed early. As they went out the door, they grabbed their lunch pails.

"Good-bye, Miss Youngren, we'll see you in the morning."

I stood on the porch till the cars disappeared in a cloud of dust, feeling like Maria in *The Sound of Music* when she was overwhelmed, yet skipped to her "appointed place." I sat down at the desk and began lesson plans. It was going to be a long night.

***

The next day was the first "real" day of school. Pauline and Nancy joined the others. The threshing crew had moved on. My long night of planning was rewarded. The individual assignments for each grade were on the blackboard. We began with arithmetic and moved on to reading. As I moved from grade to grade, I was amazed at how diligent they were— eager to please, just "good kids." I wondered, would the good behavior last, in the classroom, with disagreements, fights on the playground…and what about discipline?!

Soon it was time for lunch. Jimmy and Bob again walked home. The other boys gathered around the broken water pump, while the girls sat on the porch steps.

The older girls were having an intense conversation when Rosemary said, "Miss Youngren, can we talk to you?"

"Oh yes," I responded as I walked over and sat on the steps with them.

"Well, last year we had a few problems," she began. I wondered what was coming next. She continued, "When someone got in trouble, the teacher kept them after school. The parents were not happy because we all have chores to do at home. We girls talked about it this summer."

"Yes," chimed in Nancy. "Could we have a Citizenship Club on Friday afternoons?"

"What did you have in mind? It sounds like you have some good ideas."

"Well, when someone gets in trouble," began Norma, "or is ornery or rude, we could bring it up in the club and decide together what to do."

Just then Mary Lou came running up. "Miss Youngren, Ike grabbed my new hair ribbon and dumped it in the water pail!"

"Here it is," Arlene added, "dripping wet, and I saw him do it!"

Quickly I surveyed the situation and tried to say confidently, "Thank you for telling me, Arlene. Hang the wet ribbon on the porch railing and we'll discuss it at our first Citizenship Club meeting this afternoon."

Mary Lou stomped off mumbling "I'll just tell Ike and he'll be sorry!"

The older girls smiled. "Can we really have our first meeting this afternoon?"

"Yes, we'd better get started right away."

So that afternoon we began. Nancy was elected president and Rosemary their secretary, who began taking notes. Arlene and Yvonne, who witnessed the "tragic event," testified. Norma suggested that Ike should lose two recesses. The class agreed. Nancy asked the class to think of a name and a class song for the next meeting. Jimmy suggested thinking of ideas for programs.

Their enthusiasm was contagious. The Citizenship Club proved a great success in controlling behavior. No one wanted the class to vote their punishment.

As the meetings progressed, so did their ideas. They began to respond to the roll call with jokes, songs, etc.

We were all so proud of Johnny, our first grader, when he read to us from his reader. Everyone clapped as he timidly smiled.

I brought books on the train from the Sheridan library for them to read and share. Some of their favorites were *My Friend Flicka*, *Tom Sawyer* and *Rebecca of Sunnybrook Farm*. They would relate the stories to the others during club time.

It was also the time we'd plan parties, programs and even field trips to Sheridan and other neighboring schools.

Friday afternoon club meetings became a unique time!

***

It was surprising how quickly our daily routine emerged. We'd begin with the pledge of allegiance. My heart filled with pride and I felt a moment of thankfulness as they stood so straight and tall, enunciating each word.

Arithmetic came first—from their individual books, one lesson at a time, precept upon precept! Jimmy, an eighth grader who showed leadership qualities, urged the eighth graders to start on their arithmetic assignments. I began with Johnny, our first grader, and moved on to the other grades.

Reading and spelling were also in the morning. Pauline Ruski, our only seventh grader, worked with the sixth and eighth grades. There were gaps in her learning, especially in arithmetic, perhaps due to changing schools. The Ruski family moved later that year, taking Pauline, Edgar and little Marie.

My schooling had been in phonics, phonics and more phonics. I believe it is the foundation for reading and spelling. The children learned to read clearly and to enunciate. The spelling words were pronounced syllable by syllable. They listened to the other students, and often helped each other. We were a family.

The afternoon classes were geography, history and science.

We began a habit that continued all through my teaching years. I sat on a desk or stool the last ten or fifteen minutes before dismissal and asked the question, "What can you say when your mother asks, 'What did you learn in school today?'" Little Marie stood up and said proudly, "I learned to say 'thank you' today."

Little Marie was a very attractive second grader, but she struggled with being very shy. When she received complements she would often hang her head and mumble. One recess we talked about responding with a simple 'thank you.' We all clapped because we were so proud of her.

Then others spoke up spontaneously, wanting to share. If we went overtime, Mr. Crackenberger and Roy Corley reminded us by honking their horns out in the schoolyard.

***

After the children left for home, I needed to deal with the heat situation. I had never built, banked or tended a fire before. My parents or older brother took care of the fire in the kitchen and the furnace—I never realized it would be a crucial part of my first job!

I shook down the ashes from the grate and deposited them in the coal bucket to carry them outside, away from the building. I remember experiencing the prairie wind blowing the ashes back in my face many times. When I returned to the coal room to get the kindling to start the fires, I realized the kindling was gone! Only a stick or two remained. Grabbing the water buckets, I hurried out to relay the news to Hedwik. She was picking beans in her garden.

She was startled to learn there was no remaining kindling.

"Jim, Bob and I spent all summer, off and on, collecting that kindling from the prairie. That was to last all year! All there is out here on the prairie is sagebrush, and you can't burn it in a stove. I don't know what we can do!" she said, very dismayed.

"Oh, Hedwik, I'm so sorry. I didn't know." I thought of my dad, who *always* had a solution, and I went on, "but that's okay. I can bring back wood every Sunday afternoon on the train. My dad will help."

So my wood problem was solved by a gunny sack of wood, which my father prepared and the conductor threw off the train, before I stepped off the train each Sunday afternoon. Thank you, Dad!

As the days became cooler with rain and snow flurries, I needed warmth in my room at night. Thus I needed to bank the fire, beginning with the paper, kindling and small coal, then large clumps of coal to burn slowly, hopefully all night. Oh yes, don't forget the damper—if open, it'll burn too fast; if closed, your room will be filled with smoke. I learned this more than once. If you wake up freezing, get up, find more kindling and coal and jump back in bed! The thermostat is a wonderful invention.

5
Halloween

Their first party! Halloween was an extraordinary time that the children wanted to share with the community in the Grange Hall. The Grange Hall was a large public building across from the school. It was used for square dances, Sunday school, Grange meetings and other events. The children were very excited. The boys decided to plan the games, the girls the refreshments, while everyone made cats, pumpkins and witches to decorate.

I realized how intent they were when Jimmy asked Rosemary, "Aren't we going to dress up for Halloween?"

Rose confidently replied, "We haven't time for that now! We'll have a dress-up day later."

Two plays emerged from the group. They voted for the one which included everyone…and was the most exciting and scary. The older girls had written it together at a recent slumber party.

That evening, as we were preparing to cross the road to the Grange Hall, Edgar Ruski began to whimper, "What if I forget, make a mistake and ruin everything?!"

Pauline gave him a hug, "It's okay, Edgar, you'll remember."

"You know, that's okay if you're a little scared or frightened," I told them as the others began to get fearful. "That shows you really want to do a good job. And you know what? *Every* good program has at least two mistakes, so it's okay."

"Are you sure, Miss Youngren?" asked Edgar.

"Oh yes, very sure. Edgar, it's going to be great."

We walked across the street together. The Grange was bursting with the children's pumpkins, cats and witches on the walls. Lighted jack-o-lanterns were everywhere as the community folks greeted one another. We had all gone over after lunch to decorate. Hedwik had gone early to light the pumpkins. What a gem she was!

During the play, Johnny, our first grader, began his lines, surveyed the crowd and froze! Edgar quickly moved to his side and whispered, "It's okay." Then looking at me, he announced, "There's the first mistake, Miss Youngren! We still have one more to go!"

I stepped up to explain. Everyone laughed and clapped as we went on with the show—that was our only mistake.

The games were the highlight of the evening. Everyone joined in—the Levi-clad and booted fathers, teenagers from town, helpful mothers, little ones running in and out and our reliable boys' committee supervising. We (yes, I joined in too) bobbed for apples in the wash tubs, ate cream pies with our hands behind our backs and ran relays, slipping on the wet floor. Ike won the cream pie eating game. He was rewarded with a crisp new dollar bill, which was delivered with pomp and circumstance.

The mothers overloaded the refreshment table with their blue ribbon cakes—chocolate with creamy chocolate frosting, lemon cake with coconut frosting, applesauce cake with caramel frosting—all made from scratch—and a large plate of chocolate brownies.

Slowly the families found their way to their trucks as the awesome full harvest moon smiled down on them. It was an evening we'd never forget.

However, the "never to be forgotten" mishap came later. I had gone home for the weekend. After I returned to Ulm with my basket of food and my gunny sack of wood, I walked to the schoolhouse, lay down my parcels and hurried outside to the "necessary." The privy was not standing up straight and tall anymore…it was lying on its side! I jiggled it, thinking perhaps the wind had blown it over and I could set it up again. No way! It was stuck!

I walked swiftly down to Hedwik's to report the news. She and the boys laughed heartily. When Mike, her husband, joined us, he said, "Oh, they do that every Halloween."

"Who is 'they'?" I said. "I don't think it's funny at all." I was visibly upset.

"Oh, it's just the neighborhood bunch of older boys who are in high school. They were just having fun," chuckled Mike as he and his boys went out to finish their chores.

I turned to Hedwik, "And just what are the children and me to do for facilities?" I said, not knowing how to discuss the situation while being encircled with waves of resentment and anger.

She smiled, "Oh, they'll take care of it before long. The children will need to take turns, girls, then boys, going outside behind the schoolhouse. It'll just be temporary. They'll be setting it up soon."

"In the meantime," she continued, as she reached toward a lower shelf, "here's an everyday commode. It's not china or painted flowers, but very light, with a lid and handle, very handy on cold nights, though."

"Thank you," I murmured as she put the enamel pail in a flour sack for me to carry back to the schoolhouse. I didn't trust myself to say more. I was only thinking of the inconvenience, plus the inconsideration of the culprits.

That night it rained. The rain turned to a heavy wet snow that covered the privy. It snowed off and on the months of November, December, January and February—snow upon snow. The first of March, they tried to set it up, but it was stuck like glue. But when

I came back from Easter weekend it welcomed me, sitting straight and tall again. It had been a long, cold, uncomfortable situation for all of us. No one ever confessed or apologized.

It was just considered "one of those things."

6
Eating Out

One of the challenging suggestions in my school agreement was to visit each of the families for an evening meal and overnight stay. This was a task I was not looking forward to—not knowing what to expect.

The only first grader was Keith Crackenberger, who was often called Johnny. He was a small, shy, bright child, who wore Levi's and cowboy boots that he would grow into someday. His father, Joe, drove him to school each morning. One afternoon, when Joe picked up his son, Johnny ran back into the schoolhouse. "Pa said we would pick you up tomorrow and stay all night cause we live a long ways. Is that okay?" he panted.

"Oh yes, that would be great," I replied as he ran out the door. As I heard his boots going down the porch steps I wondered how it would be, for I had never met his parents.

The next afternoon, we squeezed in the ranch truck smelling of hay and horses. The truck creaked and whined as we drove along the endless miles. Joe was a lean, lanky older man in his late sixties or seventies, a rancher from way back. He related that his wife, Johnny's mother, was from Norway. His first wife had passed away. It was a long, dusty ride before we saw the ranch sitting alone on the prairie—sagebrush, barn, corrals—no trees. He introduced me to Ruth, who was tall, blonde and young; I knew we would have a good time together. She walked me around the ranch, proud of their layout—the cow, chickens and handsome horses. Johnny got on his horse and galloped around the barn. Ruth laughed quietly as we watched his antics.

After a scrumptious evening meal, she lit the lamps and told me of her home in Norway, showing me the pictures of her family and homeland. We chuckled and talked until midnight.

Next morning, very early, we had breakfast. First we had a steaming bowl of oats, then bacon, eggs and pancakes, with a large juicy T-bone and fried potatoes. We laughed, ate and put the T-bone in a bag for lunch, and set off reluctantly for school.

We were late! I hurriedly ran in to start the fire in the cold stove. It coughed, sputtered and smoked, for I'd forgotten to open the damper. The children played outside while I opened all the windows that weren't painted shut. Jimmy came running in to tell me that Mrs. Conley had just driven up.

"Who is she?" I asked.

"She's the state superintendent of schools," he replied.

She had stopped on her way to give exams at Dutch Creek. I introduced myself and explained the circumstances. She quickly took over. Sending the children out to the playground, she told me to go in my room and change my smoky clothes while she got the fire going. She told me she had experienced damper trouble many times in her years of rural teaching.

When the children came in, she taught the arithmetic lesson to the five eighth graders at the table by the south window, with the sun streaming in, as the classroom became warmer. I gathered the younger ones around the stove, holding little Marie on my lap, as she was whimpering from falling up the steps earlier. Later, Mrs. Conley checked the inventory of the textbooks. At lunchtime, we sat together on the porch and she shared her school experiences.

She left promising to return later in the year to give the state exams. The children waved goodbye and followed her out to her car. What an elegant, down-to-earth person she was.

The next place I went for supper was the Pence family. Their dad, a handsome, weathered rancher in his Levi's, boots and hat, picked me up after school along with the three girls, Norma, Yvonne and Betty Lou. We sat in the back of the pickup on old blankets as he drove over the dirt roads to the ranch. When we stepped into their warm, comfortable home, the girls showed me their room with all their treasures, a special doll, rock collections, etc. Betty Lou chatted away most of the supper hour in their large, homey farm kitchen. We had fried chicken and cauliflower with fresh peas and a cream sauce. It was so good. I'd never had that combination before. Perhaps it was the fresh garden vegetables, plus the rich cream and homemade butter. No overnight, but I knew then why Mrs. Pence was considered such a good cook!

Betty Lou, Mr. Pence and I crowded into the cab of the pickup and arrived at the schoolhouse in time to turn on the kerosene lamp. I can't remember having a flashlight that year.

Somehow I never got around to visiting the other homes, although later, I often visited the Corleys. But that's another story!

7
Ray

It had been a slow, sleepy Monday morning, but now it was time for lunch, a favorite time, just relaxing with our lard lunch pails on the porch. Mom had given me one grey lunch pail, with LARD in bright silver letters on the front.

I glanced at Rose, Pauline, Norma and Nancy, all grouped together.

"Rose, those brownies look so good! Does your mother like to bake?"

Before she could answer, her brother Ike broke in, "Our mom is dead and so is our pa. Rose makes our brownies." He dashed off to join Bob on the playground.

"Oh, I'm sorry, Rose, I didn't know."

"That's okay, Miss Youngren. My dad died first and then my mom got cancer."

"And Rose took care of her before she had to go to the hospital, and I helped sometimes," offered Nancy.

"Rose can bake good bread, too," added Pauline.

"That's great," I said hesitantly, for I was at a loss for adequate words.

Mary Lou came running up the steps. "Miss Youngren, will you make the boys play Red Rover with us?"

"Yes, I think that would be fun. Let's all play!"

The boys grumbled till Ike hollered, "Boys against the girls! Come on, guys!"

They formed their lines. Jimmy was the boys' captain, Rose the girls'.

"Red Rover, Red Rover," said Jimmy, "We dare Miss Youngren to come over."

I ran hard to break through their line; however, they "double held," so I ended up joining their line.

"That's okay, Miss Youngren," shouted Mary Lou. "We'll get you back!"

We ran overtime that noon, then headed for the water bucket and filed in to listen to *The Secret Garden* with their sweaty heads down on their cool desktops.

***

It was Tuesday morning at the Corleys' ranch. Ray, the older brother, called out, "Rosemary, Ike, hurry it up. We're running late."

They ran out, slamming the screen door.

"Be careful with that screen door, guys! It's about to fall off its hinges!"

They piled in the cab of Ray's well-worn pickup with their lunch pails. Off they went in a whirl of dust.

Ray was a quiet, handsome man. It hadn't been easy for him to keep things going at the ranch since his parents were gone. His brother Chuck went to high school in Sheridan, coming home on the week-ends to help with the ranch work. Rose would soon be a teenager, going to high school next year. Being patient and helpful to Rose as she attempted all the household chores and trying to be a father to nine-year-old Ike was a big responsibility for a twenty-four-year-old man.

Ray's injured feet made him walk with a limp. Often he found himself very tired at the end of the day, wondering if he'd remembered everything. In his gentle, helpful manner he quietly showed his love and concern for Rose and Ike.

As Ray was driving slowly home from the schoolhouse he began to ponder. How he wished for a good ol' ranch breakfast with bacon and eggs and even pancakes like his mom used to make. Breakfast for them now was a hurried cold cereal meal with fresh milk and thick cream from yesterday's milking.

As the truck lurched over the washboard road, he smiled. Maybe he should go into town and find a wife. However, he didn't even know a gal in town! He could visualize a Sunday dinner—Chuck, Rose, Ike and himself enjoying mashed potatoes, fried chicken, biscuits and apple pie—how long had it been?

8
The Dance

It was Friday—lunchtime on the front steps of the schoolhouse.

The older girls, Norma, Rose, Pauline and Nancy, were talking enthusiastically. I moved a little closer.

"Oh yes," said Pauline, "My big sister Rosie is bringing her friend Ruth from town because Georgie likes her. He met her at the Dutch Creek dance."

"How long will Georgie be home from the Army?" asked Norma. And then she said slowly, "I don't think we can come, although Eugene will be there with Chuck and the guys."

"Oh, good," chimed Rose, "I want to dance with Eugene.

That Saturday night, two of the teen-aged girls in the neighborhood—Rosie Ruski and her friend Ruth—arrived at the Corleys' house to deliver some beer for the party at the Grange.

As the girls sat in the Corleys' kitchen, Ray, Rose's older brother, came into the house mumbling, "Those cows broke through the fence again!"

He pulled off his shirt, baring his chest, not taking notice of the girls.

Walking over to the washstand, he dipped water from the bucket and added some from the tea kettle. He began to shave. Ruth looked away, unaccustomed to this behavior, as she lived in town with indoor plumbing. Ray was oblivious to the girls.

"Oh, Rose," he said to his sister, "did you get my shirt ironed today?"

"No, Ray, but you can wear this one," Rose replied as she handed it to him.

"Thanks, Rose. Those brownies were great, but they're about gone!"

"That's okay. I'll bake some more tomorrow."

Ruth was beginning to feel uncomfortable and nudged her friend, saying, "I think we'd better go." Then she turned to Ray's sister, "Don't forget to take the beer to the Grange, Rose."

***

Later that evening, at the Grange, Ruth, who loved to dance every dance, had to sit down. The only available seat was next to Ray on the sidelines against the wall.

"You're quite the dancer, Ruth," Ray began.

"Yes, I really like to dance…but I didn't like it tonight when you got ready right in front of us at your place," she replied.

"Oh, well, I heard you were Georgie's girl so I didn't even notice."

"Well, I'm not Georgie's girl. I don't even like him." She paused. "Care to dance?"

"No, I don't dance. I was born with crippled feet. I've had a couple surgeries. Well, they're just unhandy. Guess that's why I'm crazy about horses. They're my feet."

Ruth smiled. She was not addicted to horses. She didn't even like horses. In fact, she was scared of them. However, she didn't think she would mention that at the moment. She surprised herself by spending the rest of the evening eating and talking quietly with Ray.

They talked about their families and the major things in their lives. Ray enjoyed his horses, his own herd of Herefords and the ranch. Ruth liked her job at the telephone office and especially liked cooking. There were seven children in her family, so there was plenty of practice.

As they rose to leave, Ray asked, "S'pose I could stop by your telephone office when I come to town and we could have lunch?"

As Ruth got into the car with Rosie, she was very quiet.

"Whatcha thinkin' about, Ruth?"

"Oh nothing—just a little tired from dancing."

"You didn't do much dancing. You spent most of the evening talking to Ray Corley."

"Yes, I s'pose," Ruth smiled as she wondered how it would be to live on the prairie, no indoor plumbing or electricity, quietness, ranch life, a different life....

Meanwhile, as Ray drove home from the dance with Rose and Ike nodding sleepily next to him in the cab, he smiled as he thought of Ruth. She was a pretty thing, dark brown ringlets, freckles sprinkled on her face—from a large family and loved to cook! How good it would be to have bacon and eggs and even pancakes, like his mother used to make.

He smiled as he turned up their road to his home. It had been a very good evening.

9
Monday

It was the Monday morning after the weekend dance at the Grange. As I rang the bell, the children scurried into the hall, hanging their wraps and shoving their lunch pails into the cubbyholes. Ike was the first one in the classroom.

"Oh, Miss Youngren, Ray has a girlfriend!"

Rose stepped up, "She's not his girlfriend! She just came to the dance with Rosie Ruski. Besides, she likes to dance and Ray can't dance at all!"

"Well, they sat and talked a long time," asserted Ike, as he sank into his desk and pulled out his books.

Soon it was lunch time; Betty Lou stepped out on the porch. "It's cold and cloudy. I don't want to eat outside."

Don and Jimmy moved the large bulky green table closer to the stove.

"That table is so great," I remarked. "I wonder who built it for us."

Don, who was usually very quiet, spoke up. "Bun Mason, he's on the school board. They don't have any kids but he's always helping us. He even painted it green for us."

Yes, green seemed to be a favorite color, I surmised as I thought of the green wainscoting encircling my room—or maybe he just had an extra can of green paint around.

I remembered meeting Bun Mason at the general store. I had asked him about his name, Bun. He grinned as he responded, "I had many older sisters. When I was born, they thought I was so cute, they called me Bunny Rabbit. In school I was Bun—so it just caught." I think his real name was Archibald or Theodore or…?

Sitting next to Rose, I unwrapped my peanut butter sandwich. I heard her quietly remark to Nancy, "Ray's going to town today. He said he thought he'd stop at Woolworth's. That's what we do when we go to town."

As the conversation continued, I said cautiously but very curious, "Is Ruth from Ulm?"

"No, she's from town," said Pauline. "She came out with my sister Rosie. They were good friends in high school."

"Oh…and her last name?"

"Ferguson, Ruth Ferguson. I really like her," she added.

My light bulb turned on! Ferguson?! My very best friend in the eighth grade was *Mary* Ferguson. She had a younger sister named Ruth, who often tagged along with us. I'd envied their large, happy family of seven brothers and sisters.

After graduation I went away to school and Mary got a job in California. Remembering our good times together, I thought how great it would be to see Ruth again! She must be 19 now!

10
Weekend I

The days hurried by and soon it was Friday. At our noon recess, the children were restless—anxious to begin their weekend plans of riding their horses, square dances at the Grange, perhaps going to town and just having their own time.

I brought out a soft baseball-sized ball.

"Hey, let's play Ante Over!"

"But Miss Youngren," said Rose, "we don't know how."

"Oh, it will be fun to learn a new game. First we need teams."

"Let's have the boys against the girls," shouted Edgar.

"Sure," chimed in Ike, "we can beat the girls!"

"But there are more girls than boys," said Don.

"We don't care," replied Ike, "we can still beat 'em."

"Okay," I said, "boys against the girls. The boys will all go to the back of the school house. The girls will stay on this side. The captain of the girls will say 'Ante Over' and throw the ball over the roof to the other side. *If* one of the boys catches it, they take the ball and run around the school house to tag the girls. The girls run to the other side. If they make it to the other side, they are safe. If not, they have to stay on the boys' team. *If* the boys don't catch the ball, they can't chase the girls, but they have to throw the ball back and call 'Ante Over.' If the girls catch the ball, they run to tag the boys. If they tag some of the boys, the tagged boys must be on the girls' team. When the game is over, the biggest team wins."

"We can tag all those girls," boasted Edgar.

And they did!

Then they ran into the school room for a drink of water, and they laid their heads down on the cool desks, as I read aloud.

Afterwards, we had Friday art class, a much anticipated time. Beginning with the instructions from the school curriculum, we all learned together. One of their favorite lessons was drawing the human body. Don Rice became our model that day. He stood straight and tall, as Jimmy took a yardstick to measure the length of his head. Then they saw how many units of measured length it took for the arms and legs in order to get the right proportions. They marked off the measured units on the soft manila paper that we used only for sketches.

Pauline asked Don if he would take a running position.

"No," said Yvonne, "I want to make my person sitting down."

"No," interrupted Rose, "let's make them all standing this time."

"Great idea, Rose," I said. "Next time someone else can be the model."

Marie raised her hand, "Please, teacher, can I be the model next time, 'cause I don't draw very good?"

"I'm sure you can, Marie, and we can help each other draw right now."

They busied themselves, each with their own drawing. They were amazingly creative. The girls' drawings were beautifully dressed with long, gorgeous hair—perhaps their dreams? The boys added jeans and cowboy boots to their drawings, for horses and boots filled their heads. Ike added a horse to his picture, and proudly proclaimed, "I'm going to take mine home today."

"Let me hang it up with the others," his sister Rose suggested.

"No, I want Ray and Chuck to see it, and I'll bring it back Monday," said Ike.

"Then I'll take mine home, too," chimed in Bob and Edgar.

The girls helped clean up the room. Mr. Pence in his truck, Ray Corley in his pickup and Johnny's dad were waiting in the schoolyard to pick up their kids. The Miechs and the Ruskis began their walk home.

"See you Monday, Miss Youngren."

"Have a good weekend!"

I turned back to the schoolhouse, put everything in order and looked forward to the train's whistle. As I walked down the road past the Miechs' and the store, I paused to join Jim, who was also going into town. He hadn't been feeling good for a while and thought he'd better see a doctor.

Jim was a gentle, kindly man. Although his smile was difficult due to his burn injuries, his smile was always there. Though I was curious about his background, including his family and so forth, his manner made it very clear that he would not disclose his life. We walked slowly up the incline as the train chugged to a screeching stop.

Ulm, the prairie and the countryside floated away as we approached Sheridan. My teenaged, blonde Swedish sisters, Sigrid and Esther, met me in Daddy's new turquoise and white Mercury.

It was good to be home for the weekend—to enjoy the luxury of a bathtub and trade my soiled clothes for fresh ones. What a gem my mother was! I washed out my old black skirt because Mama's routine wash day was *all day* Monday. Proudly and patiently, my dad had "dug out" a basement to equip Mama with a laundry room. It was a long arduous task as he carried out bucket by bucket of dirt after he came home from his work on the Burlington railroad. We were so proud when Dad put in the small laundry stove that held the shiny copper boiler that boiled the sheets and white things each Monday. Then with a wooden pole, Mama would transfer the clothes to the washing machine. After they were washed in the machine, she would put them through the wringer, into the liquid bluing (whitening solution) rinse water. Next the clothes went through the wringer again and were deposited in the clothes basket. The basket was carried upstairs and the clothes were hung on the clothesline.

Wash day was truly an all-day routine on Mondays. And of course we used Oxydol, so we could get an extra dish for our kitchen set. A prime family time was listening to the "Ma Perkins Oxydol" soap opera on the radio at noon.

One time when I went home, "the old black skirt" didn't get washed out, so I wore my Sunday dress. Mary Lou Pence greeted me the following Monday, very dismayed, and exclaimed, "Oh Miss Youngren, where is your 'old black skirt?'" Thus it received its name.

On another trip home, a new green blouse lay on the sewing machine. "That's for you, Sis. Bring two blouses home each week and you'll have two to take back."

"I like it! And they are all the same pattern. The black and white checked has been my favorite, but this one is neat! Thanks so much, Mom."

How simple life was in those days—one bucket of water a day—two blouses and a skirt each week—how different from today.

The weekend flew by with "Youth for Christ" in the town's auditorium on Saturday night, seeing everyone at church on Sunday and Sunday dinner with the family. We'd have either fried chicken from our hen house or a roast with browned potatoes and carrots.

Then we piled in Daddy's shiny Mercury (we would spend all day applying Johnson's paste wax and then rubbing till it shined) to take me to the train station. I was accompanied by a gunny sack of wood for the week and a basket of home cooked food, which didn't have a kerosene smell.

When I boarded the train, I saw Jim at the end of the train cars. I walked down to sit with him. He was very somber.

"How was your trip, Jim?"

He smiled wearily, "Well, I found out that I can't afford to die. I went up to Champions Mortuary." Then he said again, "I can't afford to die, and after working hard all my life, the county is not going to bury me. I'll just keep on plugging for a while."

I said nothing, as there was nothing to say, but I patted him on his shoulder and covered his scarred hand with mine as we sat together in silence.

Only too soon the conductor came by and said, "Ulm is the next stop." He picked up my gunny sack of wood and threw it off as the train shrieked to a stop. Jim and I got off and waved to the conductor, picking the sack up together. "See you next week."

We walked slowly toward the store as the sun was setting.

11
Watermelon Hill

One fall morning, Bob came running up the steps, "Miss Youngren, my mom and Jimmy are bringing watermelons from our garden for our lunch today! Here they come!"

"Oh, thank you," I told Hedwik. "Won't you come and eat with us at noon?"

"Not today. Mike and I need to go to town. Another time, perhaps."

The melons were round and firm. We placed the bushel basket in the hall until lunch time.

As we carried them to the porch, Jimmy suggested, "Miss Youngren, they're real juicy, and, well, pretty messy. We better not eat on the porch."

"Let's go up on the hill and have lunch," Edgar said, pointing to the rounded hill east of the schoolhouse.

"Settle down, Edgar, we've never done that!" admonished his sister.

"Then let's do it! Can we, Miss Youngren?"

"Let's give it a try. Everyone help carry the melons, and let's go."

Soon we were at the top, and not in a hurry to settle down.

"Look," said Bob, "we can see my house and the barn, and there's our dog."

They surveyed the area, feeling like "the king of the hill" before they settled down for lunch and the ripe melons.

We split the melons on the rocks, spit the seeds and ate the melons down to the rind, then rolled the rinds down the hill.

"Look," said Johnny, "mine went the farthest."

"Yep, you're the winner," Don said as he patted him on the shoulder.

No one wanted to leave. We lay back in the grass and watched the clouds roll by, imagining all kinds of shapes.

As we tramped down the hill, Rose suggested, "Let's call it Watermelon Hill." There was a resounding "Yeah, Watermelon Hill!"

***

That evening I began report cards. The grade book was in the top drawer of my desk. I dreaded opening it, for only the names of the pupils were there, no grades. I never liked grades.

I remembered being in grade school, always in the middle group. I wasn't in the smartest group, the eagles, who seemed very confident in most everything, or the lowest group, who had difficulty with many things. I was in the bluebirds, not exceptionally smart, not too dumb, just medium. I have always been "just medium" in about everything, maybe boring, but very comfortable.

My Mom called it "happy medium." She applied it to every area of life. For example, in religion, don't worry about the "Holy Rollers" in the big tent down by the railroad track who shouted and sang at night, or the 5 a.m. early mass. Just walk to Sunday school each Sunday morning and "mind your P's and

Q's." (Always wondered about P's and Q's, but we didn't ask!)

Don't eat like a pig at Thanksgiving and Christmas; have a peanut butter sandwich before you go and help yourself politely to a little bit of everything. Be not too fat, or too skinny, "just medium." I like "happy medium." Abraham Lincoln said, "God must have liked the common people because he made so many of them." I like the term, "happy medium" better than common people, though.

Back to the grade book and report cards....Each child was different. Everything came very easy for Jimmy. Bob, his brother, tried, but it was more difficult. Each child was an individual, and I wanted to stimulate and encourage each one. Consequently, I emphasized their improvement—with encouragement—nothing derogatory, and no grades. So...no grades in the grade book.

I did the report cards, and they looked grand, mostly A's and B's. I sent them home the next afternoon, telling them how proud I was of each one of them for trying hard and doing their best. (By my later years in elementary school in town, grades had given way S's and U's, which meant Satisfactory and Unsatisfactory.)

Later in the afternoon, there was a knock at my classroom door. Hedwik had brought up two buckets of water and placed them in the hallway so I wouldn't need to get the water later.

"Come in, and thank you so much for the water. Did you see the report cards?"

"Yes, that's why I stopped in. The children stopped in the post office to get their mail and wanted to show their report cards."

"Oh, that was good." I hesitated, "Was everyone happy?"

"Yes, that's why I stopped by. May I sit down?"

Sensing that she was "on a mission," I invited her to sit at the green study table where the sun was sending its last warm rays.

She proudly and firmly told me that she had been a teacher, and that definite grades were definitely important. If a child missed four spelling words from a list of ten, that was 60%, or a C. She continued, her Jimmy had always been a straight-A student, as it came naturally for him. Bob had some problems, but he usually tried. Children and their parents need to know who they are, what they are capable of doing, accept it early in life and do their best. (I remembered being a bluebird as far back as first grade!) I sadly thought of the children and parents who pushed and expected more and more, never really accepting their child.

I knew she was right. I had seen the situation in my own family. I didn't fully realize that *you can't expect from others what they are unable to give... socially, intellectually, physically, musically and mathematically*. Each one is a precious individual.

With tears in my eyes, I rose to thank her. "You'll do fine," she responded. "The boys really look forward to coming to school each day. Well, almost every day," she laughed, as she patted my shoulder. (That seemed to be the accepted "touching" at that time.)

As she left, missing my water walk due to her kindness, I sat on the porch steps…I cried for being so stupid, I cried wondering how the children would feel getting "real" report cards and I cried because I was so glad to be right there.

The sun was slowly sinking out of sight. I went to my desk and began to plan a NEW day.

12
The Blizzard

It was a very cold snowy day. The north wind had blown steadily all night and the snow swirled as the snowflakes chased each other in a mad flurry.

The Ruski children—the seventh-grade smiling Pauline, third-grader Edgar, and little Marie—arrived at school a little later than usual. They'd had a long walk through the snow storm.

"It wasn't snowing when we left," Pauline explained apologetically, as if she had caused the snow. She was a sweet blonde girl, always there to watch over Edgar, who was a mischievous elf, and Marie, a small, quiet, fragile little girl. Their cheeks were red and chapped. Only Marie had a scarf, which was covered with snow. Edgar had lost his mittens. They huddled around the stove, slowly removing their wraps. They shivered as the snow fell from their clothes and melted into puddles around the stove.

The other children began to arrive. Mr. Pence brought the three girls—Norma, Yvonne and spunky Mary Lou—to school in his truck. Mary Lou was upset with the cold and snow and grumbled most of the morning. Jimmy and Bobby had trudged up the road in the snow as it continued. Ray Corley brought Rose and Ike in his pickup. They were excited about the snow as it began to make drifts.

"Maybe we'll get snowed in!" Ike said as he took off his coat and shook the snow till it made new puddles on the floor.

As they huddled around the stove to get warm, they began to tease one another with their icy hands and to throw the snow, which was caked on their boots and wraps. Not wanting an uproar, I clapped my hands and explained, "Move your desks closer to the stove and we'll get started." Slowly, like molasses, they meandered to their desks and began their assignments.

Soon it was time for lunch. Johnny, Don and the Childress girls did not brave the storm that day. Large, fluffy snowflakes were still falling. We ate together at our green study table, except for Jimmy and Bob, who walked home to a hot lunch, with Bob complaining about going out in the cold and snow. Mrs. Pence had baked the night before. It was common to start baking when a storm was coming. She packed extra goodies, which the girls shared with us. Pauline opened their family lunch pail and gave Edgar and Marie thick slices of homemade bread with a thin frosting between the slices.

"That looks so good, Pauline, what is the filling?" I asked. She blushed and said, "Oh, I put cocoa and water between the slices."

"That sounds delicious. Did you add a little sugar?"

"Oh, no, my father takes all the sugar stamps to the bar and exchanges them…he's not working now."

"Oh," I replied quickly, "Your mom really makes scrumptious bread."

She smiled and said, "I make the bread."

"You certainly do a good job, Pauline," I said, wishing I had never mentioned the bread. It seemed Mr. Ruski was working odd jobs off and on.

One Monday, much later, they did not arrive at school, so I inquired of the other children.

"They moved again," said one of the Pence girls. I really missed that family.

Hedwik Miech appeared at the school door. "The storm is getting much worse," she said. "You can hardly see the road. The Ruski children have a very long walk. It would be best if they stayed here tonight." Edgar, Ike and Bob jumped in their seats with exuberance.

"But won't their mother worry?" I protested. "And what about the Corley children?"

"No, they'll understand. We've had these storms before," she said confidently. The older girls smiled at each other in anticipation. Just then we heard a truck outside. Mr. Pence had come to pick up his daughters. The girls groaned and reluctantly bundled up to face the cold.

"Jimmy and Bob, come home with me now and we'll bring up blankets and food for the night."

The others enjoyed the blackboard, playing Tic-Tac-Toe and Hangman. When the Miechs arrived with hot homemade vegetable soup, fresh baked rolls and cookies, we all gathered around the study table to eat in the light of our two kerosene lamps as we played Twenty Questions. We laughed and talked, oblivious to the howling wind. Hedwik joined in as we played I Spy and Button, Button, Who's Got The Button, using a piece of chalk, as no one had an extra button. Edgar and Ike were going home with the Miechs for the night so they began to pull on their boots, anticipating their new adventure.

The girls carried the blankets and pillows into my room. They giggled and talked as they made their beds on the floor next to the stove. As I brought out my flannel pajamas, I said, "If you'd known you were going to spend the night, you could have brought your pajamas."

"Oh, Miss Youngren," said Pauline, "I've never had pajamas. We just sleep in our clothes."

"Well, I have another pair at home, so you can just take these with you when you go home tomorrow." She thanked me quietly.

I covered little Marie on my cot, which was placed close to the stove. I put in more coal, knowing I would be adding more during the night. After brushing the snow from inside the window sills and attempting to peer out at the drifts, I told them all goodnight and settled in with Marie, who had fallen asleep to the sound of the blowing wind.

The next morning, armed with my snow shovel, I stepped out the door. The snow had ceased to fall during the night. The wind had subsided and fresh snow blanketed everything. It was beautiful! The air was clear and cold against my face. Soon the porch and steps were cleared. My skin prickled as the icy wind began to blow, drifting the snow.

Inside, the girls had dressed and found the cold cereal and frozen milk. Since it was cold outside, the milk was kept on the window sill. Soon the fire was going strong. I remembered Hedwik's reassuring words as she'd left, "Don't worry about tomorrow. Ray can take the Ruskis home as soon as it clears up and you can catch the train."

We waited, knowing we'd all be going home soon. I wondered if this would happen again. Was this the real beginning of winter on the prairie? The wind howled and rattled the windows, reminding me who was in control.

13
The Weekend II

The school day was over. As the children were dismissed, Johnny got in the truck with his dad, the three Pence girls piled in the pickup, Ike and Rose roared off with Ray, Don's mother picked him up and Jimmy and Bob chased each other down the road. The Ruski family was lingering. Edgar had run to the john while Marie and Pauline waited with me on the porch, ready to begin their long walk home.

"Do you like to go home?" Pauline asked.

"Oh, yes," I replied. "I take my laundry and my food basket home. The schoolhouse is very quiet and lonely when all of you are gone," I added as I gave little Marie a hug.

Just then Edgar appeared. "C'mon girls, let's get home. I'm hungry! He started down the road. With a last look at the schoolroom, I shut the door securely and walked briskly to catch the four o'clock train. (There was never a key.)

Settling in the comfort of the train and putting my feet on the opposite seat, I watched as Ulm faded away. Trains had always been a comforting part of my life. The call boy used to come and bang on the screen door at home, "Iver, Iver, you need to take number 43 to Gillette today, it's a load of sugar beets."

When I was a child, I would run to the door and say, "He's coming, Jake, just a minute." There were no phones, no regular runs for my dad. As a fireman, shoveling coal into the engine, he was on call when they needed him. Jobs were scarce during those Depression years.

As the years progressed and the union became prominent, my dad did not join, resulting in hazing, "Hey, Ole, go back to Sweden, you belong back in the ole country," etc. Things got better and when I was in high school he became the engineer on the passenger train. I still have his engineer's gold watch and watch fob.

The Burlington Route Railroad was good to us and dad was a good saver. He took several trips to Sweden to visit his parents. While I was in college, he took his new Mercury and his family on the USS Stockholm.

Since we received free passes on the train, we went to California to see Uncle Oscar and his family in the summer, sleeping in the train's sleeper at night. The children slept in the top bunk, undressing and re-dressing in the cramped quarters, then falling asleep to the rhythm of the train as it click-clacked on the track.

Yes, the train played a significant part in my life, living by the railroad on the wrong side of the tracks, listening to the whistle and the chug-chug of the engines all through the night. The sudden jerk of the train stopping interrupted my train musings as I climbed down to greet my dad at the station. Only too soon it was Saturday morning at home.

"Mom, where's the baloney? I have the bread but can't find the baloney."

Her voice came from the bedroom, "It's in the fridge on the back porch. Why do you need it?"

"Remember, Mom, it's my turn to have the church kids over, so I'm making sandwiches. Where's the grinder?"

"Just look around; you had it last," she replied as she wandered into the kitchen, dressed, except for her feet, which were reluctant to give up her comfy, warm slippers for a busy day.

Later, as I ground the baloney, added the Miracle Whip salad dressing and pickle relish and finished with a flourish of lettuce, I wondered if Albert would be coming that evening. Albert was one of the steady fellows in our group. Our parents were both immigrants—his from Poland, mine from Sweden. He was tall and quite shy, with dark brown hair and eyes. I liked him.

Before I left for Ulm, he had asked me to go to a movie on a Sunday evening. My mother reluctantly agreed. After the movie, we walked to Louie's for hamburgers. Louie had a kitchen tucked behind a regular store on Main Street. As we sat on the stools, Albert laid a quarter on the counter and said, "What would you like?" I quickly calculated…hamburgers were a dime, cokes a nickel. "Let's each have a hamburger and share a coke."

"Good," Albert smiled, and added, "Lots of onions and two straws, please."

Around seven, the group began to come, one by one, including Albert, sitting on the sofa, chairs and floor, as they shared the Luther League lesson. Then Clifford, the church organist, went to the piano in the music room. It had been a bedroom previously, but when we got our attic bedrooms, dad made the doorway into an arch going into the music room, where he made out his receipts for the renters as they dropped by to pay the rent.

We all pushed back the dining room table, moved the chairs to the porch, and with the piano sounds of Glenn Miller and Bing Crosby, we jitterbugged to "Jeepers Creepers," "Boogie Woogie Bugle Boy," "Chattanooga Choo Choo," and slowed down with "Star Dust" and "In the Mood." The evening passed too quickly. We pushed back the table on the linoleum, and brought back the chairs. Mom brought out the sandwiches and cherry Kool-Aid, and we wandered out to the front steps. One by one, they left. Albert lingered. He was reporting back to the Army on Monday. He gave me his new address. I wanted to hug him, kiss him, tell him to hurry back...he was bashful, I was restrained. I certainly didn't want to be demonstrative, with Mom waiting on the front steps. I waved as he drove out the drive-way.

As we cleaned up, I said, "Mom, the sandwiches are all gone and I'm still hungry."

"Just get a slice of baloney and bread and get to bed," she replied. I folded the slice of baloney in the fold of the Rainbow bread and started up the stairs to the attic bedrooms. (Sliced, white, Rainbow bread was the smoothest thing then!)

Our attic was a very special place…a gift from my ingenious dad. When I was ten, my mother had two "change of life" babies. Well, that's what the church ladies called that incident. It seemed to be very common in those days. So, we needed more bedroom space. Dad was an inventive and ambitious man who had already sliced off an indoor bathroom between the bedroom and kitchen, with a lovely bath-tub for Saturday nights, if you emptied the water on the trees outside—bucket by bucket. You certainly didn't let the water go down the drain! He also built, in the back, a porch with a stairway going down to the basement he had dug out, bucket by bucket, for a furnace and laundry room for Mom.

Earlier, in the 1920s, like many folks in the town, he had purchased a house from the coal mines, which were bankrupt and wanted at least a hundred dollars cash for the miners' homes. Then Dad began building add-ons and attics. We were ready for the attic!

Dad built a ladder stairway in the dining room, very narrow in order to leave the large, square furnace grate uncovered in that room. That was all he could afford to do at first, so I pretended. I would go up the stairs, alone, sit on the steps and visualize how lovely it was going to be.

No one borrowed money. "Loan" was an unacceptable word, and you certainly didn't dare touch your savings. So we saved in a coffee can till the day came to break through the ceiling, which eventually resulted in two bedrooms and an even smaller play room. The play room had an ample window, with a hinge, leading to a slanted roof. We often sat on the rooftop to watch the day slowly end as the stars came out to wish us good night.

14
Spring

Spring on the prairie...the snow was gone, the blizzards were past, the sun was shining, the playful warm wind blew the sagebrush, inviting us to enjoy!

The first big event was CHOIR DAY in Sheridan! It was for all the urban schools in the county to come to the Sheridan High School to sing together. The nearby schools of Piney, Dutch Creek, Clearmont, Ucross, Cabin Creek and many more would be there. All the eighth graders in the area would be going to Sheridan High School in September, so it was a great time to meet their future classmates. Everyone was excited as they anticipated the event. The county sent us the names of the songs for us to memorize and sing all together as a large group. The songs were "America," "Wyoming," "When it's Springtime in the Rockies" and "Home on the Range." For penmanship, the children wrote the words to each song to practice at school and at home. We especially worked on enunciating each word.

"Can't we practice more at school, Miss Youngren," asked Don, "We have chores to do at home."

"I know, Don, and you're a good helper at home. What chores do you do?"

"I feed the chickens, burn the trash, milk the cow and lots of things," he added.

"Maybe you can sing to the chickens and the cow and even sing when you round up the cattle on your horse."

He smiled, "Okay, Miss Youngren, I'll try."

Several afternoons later, as I took my walk down the road for the two pails of water, I stopped at the post office for a game of checkers with Jim, the storekeeper. I hadn't won a game all year! He was an expert checker player.

Don's parents, Mr. and Mrs. Rice, dropped by the post office to pick up their mail.

"Miss Youngren, I wanted to talk to you," Mrs. Rice said softly.

"Me, too," protested her husband, "I can sing "Home on the Range" in my sleep and I say every word," he laughed hoarsely.

Mrs. Rice continued, "Can't they do that singing in school?"

"Yes, we do, but I don't want to take too much time from their regular studies. The county exams will be soon and we want our school to do really well."

"You're right, and we want to do well at the Choir Day, too, so we'll just keep singing to the chickens," chuckled Mrs. Rice.

Jim spoke up, "Those kids come in singing every day. I told Bob I could sing with them but he told me I couldn't mumble, I'd have to enunciate!" He laughed as he jumped my last man on the checkerboard.

I walked back to the schoolhouse with my two buckets of water from the Miechs' well, feeling thankful that Jimmy would bring an extra bucket in the mornings on the hot days.

***

I begin to feel uneasy about the coming Choir Day. I felt very incompetent about singing. In grade school programs, I was assigned to turn the pages for the pianist.

I once asked the teacher, "How come I always turn the pages?"

She replied, "Oh, Edna, you are such a good page turner!" Later in college, when everyone sang the "Messiah" at Easter, the instructor asked me to "mouth the words." (My musical husband told me later in life that I was a monotone.) With my lack of confidence and inability to carry a tune, I truly hoped the children would do well. And they did!!

On Choir Day, Mrs. Pence and Mrs. Miech took us to Sheridan in their pickups.

The children practiced all morning with all the other county rural schools. At noon, we all received a free lunch before walking down the hill to the Sheridan City Park to enjoy the teeter-totter, the bars, slide and swings. As the children played and talked with their new eighth-grade friends, who would be with them in school in September, the girls—Norma, Rose and Nancy—eyed the new boys and our boys—Don and Jimmy—looked over the new girls.

At 1:30 the formal program began with adults flooding the high school auditorium. The program featured the Sheridan County Choir, all singing together, then individual schools performing. It included the "Ulm Rhythm Band" playing "Lightly Row" without one mistake! The children enjoyed watching the performances of all the different schools. It was a long day.

We stopped at the Dairy Queen for chocolate cones to enjoy on our trip home. Johnny remarked, "That was fun!" and we all agreed.

15
Piney and Clearmont

Piney was a nearby school that celebrated a music festival every spring. When they invited our school, they asked us to bring three special numbers, including our "rhythm band," which had been the talk of the town since Choir Day.

"Can we all go?" asked Betty Lou.

"Ruth or Ray can take us in the pickup," ventured Ike.

"And I'm sure my Mom will drive, too," Jimmy added.

"Yes, I'm sure we can all go. We need to think about two more numbers."

"Jimmy is really getting good on the piano," offered Nancy. Nancy seemed to have an increasing interest in Jimmy since the Sheridan Choir trip. He was growing tall, had a helpful demeanor, not to mention his blond hair, sparkling blue eyes and ready smile.

"My mom says he's improving a lot on the piano," added his brother Bob.

"Would you do that, Jimmy?"

"Oh, sure. I'll let you know what I'll play," he smiled confidently.

"So we need one more number."

"Miss Youngren," Rose said softly, "Nancy, Norma and I have been singing "Paper Doll" and "Don't Fence Me In"….do you s'pose…?"

"And Jimmy could accompany us on the piano," interrupted Nancy.

Jimmy grimaced, "I would need the music."

"Oh, I have it," Norma said.

"Well," he said slowly, "I'll talk it over with my Mom."

"Good," I responded, "now let's get on with our lessons."

It was a beautiful, breezy, spring day as we left for Piney. I rode in the cab of the Corleys' pickup as Ruth told me about their wedding plans. They were planning a quiet family wedding at the Open Bible Chapel on Main Street in Sheridan in the evening. They were not sure about the exact date. Ruth was very excited, knowing it would be a whole new way of life with no indoor plumbing, no phones, a ready-made family of Rose and Ike, horses (not her favorite) and many adjustments. But when you're young and in love....

The five eighth graders rode in the back of the Corleys' pickup while Ike, Bob and the younger ones rode with Mike and Hedwik.

The Ulm Rhythm Band was in top form. Jimmy played "Humoresque" on the piano and the girls sang "Don't Fence Me In." We ate hot dogs, chips and apple pie with the Piney folks. No one wanted to leave. Finally Hedwik mentioned that it was time for chores, so we headed home.

***

Clearmont, a neighboring community, was presenting a play called "The Would Be Gentleman." We'd all heard about it at the Choir Day in Sheridan. The older girls were especially excited about going in the evening to see a real play, plus Hedwik said she and Mike would drive.

Thus the Corleys, Rose and Ike, the Childress girls, Nancy and Arlene, the Miech boys, Jimmy and Bob, the older Pence girls, Norma and Yvonne, and I piled in the back of the Miechs' pickup and hit the road to Clearmont. We were all eager to experience the thrill of this special time together.

For some reason, the scene when the servants in the play bowed to the "Monte rajah" was very impressive, according to Norma's account in the yearbook report. Perhaps the Indian culture and the servants bowing was a new concept, far different from their ranch life. They replayed that scene many times while "hanging around" together.

It was late when we piled in the pickup to go home. The ride was rough, due to the ruts from the melting snow. My "pickup pillow" helped relieve the bumps. The gentle wind blew in our faces and rumpled our hair as we lay back waiting for the moon and stars to come out. The old blankets and quilts felt warm and cozy as we crowded together.

Rose sat up quickly. "Look, everyone, there's the very first star!"

"I don't see it," said Ike, her brother.

"Right over there," she pointed.

"Oh, yeah, and here comes another."

"There's another....and two more!" added Bob.

"I counted ten," said Ike, "they're coming everywhere!"

We lay back on our blankets in awe. That was my first "counting the stars as they come out" experience. I have played it many times since with family and friends. Even now, as I sit on my front porch to count the stars, one by one, I remember that first time, 66 years ago in Ulm, lying in the back of the pickup.

16
Exams

It was May first. The eighth graders were just ready to give a geography report, when a sound was heard in the hallway. I opened the door, and there was Mrs. Conley, the county superintendent! She was a tall, large-boned, middle-aged lady with dark hair and a cheerful smile. She had dropped in on us one cold winter day early in the year and helped me get the stove started. Now she was back to give the state exams to the children in the first six grades.

Anxiety swept over me. Had the children had a good breakfast? Had they had a good night's sleep? I wondered why we weren't notified, though perhaps the anticipation of the exams would have meant a sleepless night?! I must trust Mrs. Conley's judgment and the parents' care. I didn't want the children to feel my anxiety.

"Come right in, Mrs. Conley. It's good to see you again. You can put your material right here on our study table. Eighth graders, go ahead with your next history assignment, which is on the blackboard.

I know you'll sit quietly while the others are taking their tests."

As the younger children looked up at me, wondering what was happening, I said softly, "Go outside to the john (it had been set up again at Easter), get a drink and we'll be all ready to work with Mrs. Conley." As they left, Mrs. Conley laid an oatmeal cookie and a new sharpened pencil on each desk.

"I'm sure you'll all do real well," she smiled.

My anxiety melted. It was going to be a good day. The morning passed slowly and quietly.

As she collected their papers, she remarked, "You all have such good penmanship."

"Oh, we really work on that," said Arlene.

"We like to write," said Yvonne.

"I am going to Dutch Creek now. You all have a wonderful summer. Perhaps I'll see you next year," Mrs. Conley said as she looked over the class.

Rose interrupted, "We won't be here next year. We're going to Sheridan High School in September!"

"Yes, but I will see all of the eighth graders when you'll meet with Clearmont, Ucross and Cabin Creek, to take the exams for high school at Clearmont.

"Oh...." The eighth graders looked at each other, and my anxiety began again.

She gathered her supplies and told us good-bye. It was almost noon.

"Let's eat a little earlier today," I suggested, wanting to get out into the sunshine.

"Miss Youngren, could we hike up to Watermelon Hill to eat?" asked Norma.

"But we don't have any watermelons," said Don.

"That's okay," answered Jimmy. "I'll run home and get a couple sandwiches for Bob and me. See you soon."

We hiked up the hill. It was a warm, breezy, spring day. We ate our lunches and talked about the coming summer and fall. I wondered what I would be doing then.

***

May 12th came very quickly. Hedwik offered to take the five eighth graders, Jimmy, Don, Rose, Nancy and Norma, to Clearmont in her pickup. I stayed with the others in the schoolroom. They did their arithmetic problems on the blackboard that day, and each one picked their favorite story to read aloud to the others. At recess we had two teams, the boys'—Ike, Bob and Johnny—and the girls' team—Arlene, Yvonne and Betty Lou. We played Red Rover and Red Light, Green Light. It was fun with just the six of them, but we all missed the Ruski family—Pauline, Edgar and little Marie.

The roads were very muddy from the melting snow, so the Clearmont bunch left the pickup for later and came home on the train. (Later, we learned they did well on the exams and Jimmy placed second in the county.)

17
The Last Field Trip

School was coming to a close. After the children left that afternoon, I picked up the two water buckets and began my walk. Setting the water buckets inside the post office, I noticed Jim, the postmaster, sorting the mail. He turned to me and said, "Miss Youngren, you have a letter." He handed it to me and continued sorting.

The letter was short. Albert had always been a man of few words.

Dear Edna,

I have met a Polish girl here at the post. Her parents came from Poland, too, so we speak Polish and English together. My parents want to meet her. So, on my next leave I will bring her home. I am glad you enjoy your teaching.

Sincerely,

Albert

Albert had always "been there." I had never thought of him finding someone else. I felt very alone. I tried to rationalize, for I was glad for him. He was a good friend, but I knew he'd never share my dream of going oversees to help and serve others. He would be content in his Polish culture. Their families often lived together, farming the land. Yet I felt a quiet sadness.

"See you, Jim," I mumbled.

"Sure, Miss Youngren, Stop by any time." I put the letter in my pocket.

Picking up my buckets, I walked across the street. Hedwik was in her yard, picking up the tumbleweeds that had blown about.

"Look, Edna, the crocuses are coming up!" I smiled. Evidently she sensed that I was low for she added, "Let's have one more field trip!"

I tried to muster some enthusiasm. "Really, Hewik, what did you have in mind?"

"Well, I've been thinking about it. School's about over, we could have a day in Sheridan."

"We went to Sheridan for Choir Day."

"I know, but we could have a tour of the creameries, the bakery, the courthouse—and we can think of some other places. When I taught school at Dutch Creek, we had a Sheridan Day. The boys and girls enjoyed it so much."

Her enthusiasm was catching.

"Come on in for a piece of pie and we can talk it over."

We sat at the kitchen table and added more places to the list. I mentioned that Don had gone to the iron works with his dad to get an iron gate and how he enjoyed watching the men with the blowtorches. My sister-in-law worked there, so perhaps we could get a tour.

"Oh, yes, I know Shirley. I'll stop by there. And I have a friend at the weather bureau, too, and the Sheridan press office is right next to it," added Hedwik.

"And lunch at the park," I suggested. "We could each bring a sack lunch."

"Oh, no, the mothers will make potato salad, sandwiches, and Mrs. Rice's chocolate cake; a real picnic, no sack lunch."

Jimmy and Bob came in from the yard. "It's getting dark, Miss Youngren."

Hedwik rose from the table. "Mike and I are going to town tomorrow to pick up seed so I'll check out some places and get back to you, Edna. Take the water buckets, boys, and walk Miss Youngren up to the schoolhouse."

My step was lighter as we all walked up the road. They left the water in the hallway as I lit my lantern. "Thank you, boys, I'll see you in the morning."

***

What a field trip it was! All the children were able to go. Everyone met at the schoolhouse early in the morning. Mrs. Pence took the girls in her car and the boys jumped in the back of Hedwik's pickup. Hedwik asked me to sit in the cab, a treat on the bumpy road! It was a cool spring day and everyone was in high spirits.

The boys sang all the way to town. "On Top of Ole Smokey" was their favorite. At the creameries, they watched the milk bottled as it came through the conveyor belt. The packaging operations in the bakery also used a conveyor belt, a new word for their vocabulary.

The blowtorches at the Sheridan Iron Works were fascinating, especially for the boys. Nine year-old Ike wanted to try a blowtorch, but the tour guide smiled and said, "Let's wait a few years."

Those trips filled the morning. Lunch was at the Sheridan Kendrick Park, named after Wyoming's famous senator. We all enjoyed the playground equipment, which was not available anywhere else. There were swings (my favorite), the teeter-totter, the merry-go-round and the extremely high slide, which the boys made very slick by going down on waxed paper. After we ate the mothers' potato salad and baloney sandwiches and finished with chocolate cake, we went to see the animals. There were peacocks, owls, coyotes and wolves, but the monkeys and the big black bear were their favorites. The bear must have had caffeine for lunch, maybe breakfast too, as he growled, rolled over and presented a good show while the children encouraged him with clapping and laughing.

The Pence car had a flat tire, so that canceled two church tours. The boys teased the girls about being so fat that they caused the flat tire!

The next stop was the weather bureau. Then we continued to the town newspaper, the *Sheridan Press*. They met the editor and a couple of reporters and observed the printing presses.

The jail was next. The children were very somber and listened carefully to the jailer, who later escorted them to the judge's chamber, where they could ask questions.

"That was awesome," said Don as we went down the courthouse steps.

"I was glad to get out of there," added Bob.

From there to the brewery and the Sheridan greenhouse, where the new spring plants were thriving. The fragrance was like a comforter covering us as the sunlight streamed through the glass, nurturing the new plants. We wanted to stay, but it was becoming very warm and everyone was tired.

So once again, we stopped at the Dairy Queen on Main Street for ice cream. It was a quiet ride home.

The children tumbled out of the cars at the schoolhouse. Sitting on the steps to await their rides home, Mrs. Pence asked them what they liked best.

They all agreed that Blackie the Bear was their favorite.

18
Ulm Yearbook

I began my story with the Ulm yearbook—found sixty-six years later—cream manila paper, tied with a black shoelace, ULM LONGHORNS printed with heavy brown crayons, the pages tattered and torn—and full of treasured secrets!

Rose and Norma each had a brother in high school and yearbooks were the big topic. Our project involved everyone; reports were assigned, language and penmanship skills were involved and it was fun! I learned some secrets from the "Who's Who?" page. Their nicknames were not secrets, though Ike expressed that he never liked his name Jon, and would like to give it away. (From a reliable source, I later heard he has a successful job in California and prefers to be called Jon now.)

Their favorite listed songs were revealing, like "Behind Those Swinging Doors," "Cigarettes, Whiskey and Wild, Wild Women," "Rye Whiskey," "Buttermilk Sky" and the milder "Springtime in the Rockies," "Wyoming," "Wedding March" and "Home on the Range."

The two older boys, Don and Jimmy, listed a boy pal and, in parentheses, a girl pal. Don listed only Rose's initials and Jimmy listed Esther Youngren, my younger blonde sister, who visited at the school-house when she and my other sister, Sigrid, had spring break. The older girls listed a boy, too, but no one recognized them. It was spring, even Arlene, our sixth grader, listed as her hobby, singing love songs. Everyone participated except Johnny, and his time will come!

Riding horses topped the list of favorite hobbies. Their favorite places were the dime store in Sheridan (Woolworth's), the Ulm Post Office and the Corleys' barn. All their school parties, programs and field trips were included and written up in their best penman-ship.

Jimmy concluded the book by addressing "What Ulm School has accomplished this year." His first sentence was a compliment to all of them: "The Ulm school has accomplished *a great deal this year.*" He went on to tell about the Citizenship Club. They were so proud of their discipline and sportsmanship.

Arithmetic was a prominent subject, art lessons became very creative and they were very aware of improvements in language. It was a good year!

19
Later

While we were taking field trips, exams, report cards, etc., Ruth and Ray had a quiet family wedding one evening at the Open Door Chapel on Main Street in Sheridan. In my mother's storehouse of homemade gifts, I found some beautiful embroidered pillowcases with flowers—with her crotchet work on the edges. I sent them home with Ike and Rose and received the following note the next morning:

Dear Edna,

The kids brot up the gift you sent. Golly! I don't know how to thank you—they're just simply beautiful! Thanks ever so much.

Gee, it really is swell being married!! You ought to try it sometime. I'm sort of getting settled here a little bit. It's sort of hard tho cause there's so much to do and I never seem to get around to anything.

The kids said you couldn't come up this week cause of it being report card week. Be sure that you get around to it next week though.

Ray's jaw is swollen this morning. I certainly hope he doesn't have the mumps. He ate a pickle a while ago so maybe he doesn't.

I went riding with Ray last nite. It wasn't too bad but I could sure think of plenty of things I'd rather do. Ray loves riding and horses so that I feel like a heathen telling him that I don't!

Better close for now, it's time for the kids to go to school.

All my love,

Mrs. Corley (that's me!)

I was glad for Ruth and Ray and for the children, Rose and Ike. Perhaps there would be confrontations, since Rose had been the kitchen queen for a long time, but that's life. And perhaps Ruth would learn to love horses. (However, the last time I saw her at Perkins for breakfast, although in her 70s, she assured me that her feelings had not changed.)

My thoughts moved on to the American Sunday School couple who came from Sheridan to hold Sunday school in Ulm and the outlying communities. The lady, Mrs. Koehler, took charge of the class in the Community Building across from the schoolhouse. She was a short, heavy-set and energetic lady. Her husband, Julius, who seemed much older, was pale and thin with white, wispy hair and gold-rimmed glasses.

Jimmy's family had attended the Sunday school, and from that interest, Jimmy began to borrow some of my biographies of early missionaries in faraway places. He began to share my dream. He'd often bring up the water buckets in the late afternoon so he could return a book. We shared the adventures of C.T. Stud in Africa and Jonathan Goforth in China— both veteran missionaries blazing the trail. As the sun began to close the day, we'd walk out to the porch steps to watch its brilliance slowly fade.

I began to wonder about the next year. What would I do? Where would I go? I needed to move on. Hedwik told me that next year, the teacher's salary would be doubled to $200 a month, fuel would be provided and there would be only five pupils. That was not my answer.

Soon, I wrote to a mission board, dreaming—with my quixotic personality—of sailing far away to help the needy, for I had my diploma and my teaching experience. I realize now that my dreams came from hearing many exciting stories from missionaries who returned home during my college years, and from having a good friend, Ingrid, whose father was killed by a lion in Africa. Ingrid was going to return to take his place. Plus, having read many challenging books, I was ready to go to help the world. My anxiously awaited reply from the mission board came quickly.

*Thank you for writing.

*You need more formal education.

*We don't consider single applications.

I was devastated. My dream was shattered. Waves of discouragement swept over me. I felt helpless, hopeless…. Nothing mattered.

I shared my disappointment with Jimmy. "Maybe later," he offered. (And much later, he went on to Wheaton College Medical School, became a doctor and did spend some time in Africa.)

But now I knew, I must go back to school, and find a man who would share my dream!

I read the letter again then I stuffed it in my pocket and walked slowly up to Watermelon Hill. I surveyed the countryside…Ulm, the post office, the Miechs' home, the schoolhouse…and what was beyond? Maybe I would never go overseas, maybe I wouldn't find a man to share my dreams, maybe…BUT, I had found my passion, my dream…. I loved to teach and wanted to teach for the rest of my life!

The sun was gone, leaving a blaze of orange as if it had done its work for the day. The moon would come out as a sentry for the night and then the stars, millions of tiny stars, each in their own place. I began to feel very insignificant, like a tiny star, but…I could shine. Perhaps I could even twinkle. And I could teach!

I started down the hill. It was okay. I knew I must go back to school and find that man who shared my dream, and teach for the rest of my life…somewhere.

Ulm Students in 1946

Our five 8th graders
Jimmy Miech and Donivan Rice
Rose Corley, Nancy Childress and Norma Pence

Arlene Childress
and Bob Miech

Ike Corley
and Mary Lou Pence

"Johnny" Crackenberger, our 1st grader

The Miech family
Donnie and Hedwik
Jimmy and Bob

Ulm Post Office
with Jim out front

Our Postmaster Jim,
playing Solitaire

The Front Cover of the Ulm Longhorns Yearbook

Rose Corley, Editor of the
Ulm Longhorns yearbook

Ray and Ruth Corley
Our Love Story

I received this penny postcard the following year from
Ruth Ferguson Corley, with the want add
from the Sheridan Press.

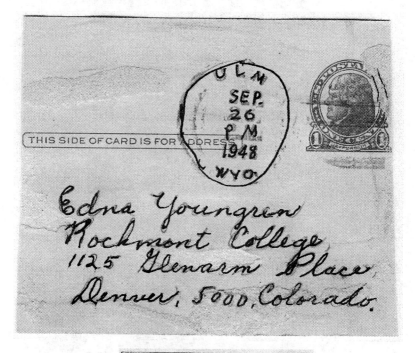

ULM
SEP.
26
P M
1948
WYO.

THIS SIDE OF CARD IS FOR ADDRESS

Edna Youngren
Rockmont College
1125 Glenarm Place,
Denver, 5000, Colorado.

BECAUSE OUR TEACHER WENT
back to college, wanted a teacher for 5 pupils. Salary $200 per
month. Living quarters and fuel
furnished. Write or call Hedwik
Miech, Ulm.   9-22

Ulm school was built in 1914, with $60.00 a month salary.
I received a $100.00 a month in 1946.
The school closed in 1968 with a salary of $387.00 a month.

The school room in 2012

The sunny classroom is in the foreground of the school house
building, with the teacherage on the other side.
The two chimneys reminded me of the two fires that had to be
constantly tended on the cold days.

Watermelon hill is in the background.
The "outdoor facilities" (john or privy)
was where the tree is standing.

Part II

Beyond Ulm

1
Moving On

I met my "prince" at Colorado Christian University in Denver. Jack had been a chaplain's assistant in Japan in World War II, and hoped to go back. He was a quiet, considerate, handsome man, and reminded me of Gary Cooper. It didn't take long for our friendship to turn to love.

Our dream of overseas ministry was hindered and halted because of health issues. When he took his physical for our marriage license, the doctor informed him, no mission board would accept him. Jack was devastated. His first thought was that we should not go ahead with the wedding; he felt he would hinder me. We cried, we prayed, we shared our grief. One of the college professors, Dr. Lapp, who had spent many years as a teacher in China, counseled and persuaded Jack to continue our wedding plans, saying our engagement diamond was our pledge.

We had a lovely Lutheran wedding in Sheridan, my home town, with my two sisters, Sigrid and Esther, as bridesmaids. Our honeymoon was in the Black Hills (where I discovered my new husband was a rock hound, resulting in returning with a trunk of rocks). Even during the wedding, there was the nagging thought of "what now?"

Jack got a job at the post office. We had three beautiful girls, Beth, Ruth and Marty. Beth's birth was difficult, resulting in brain damage and seizures, which presented a real challenge. I took night classes at UNC in Denver so I could learn about her condition. Knowing I would now need two more years of college to ever teach again, I also enrolled in other education courses. Campus attendance was required for the degree, so the three girls (ages 3, 5 and 7) and I went up to Greeley, with Jack coming on weekends. That fall, we all marched off to school together from our home in Golden, Colorado.

I taught in elementary school in Jefferson County for 27 years—at Pennington Elementary in Wheat Ridge, Colorado. Those were the Camelot years, with family trips, camping, 4-H fairs, square dancing and school. Jack had wonderful opportunities to travel to Russia, Egypt and Israel. We began supporting young missionaries from our church. They were like family.

Beth had auburn, curly hair and blue eyes. The teachers in Special Ed are superior people and she had the best. Her learning capacity was 3rd, 4th grade level with erratic behavior due to her brain damage at birth, plus seizures were frequent. Jack and I, Ruth and Marty covered her with love. She liked embroidery (we all have unique cross-stitch pieces), latch hook, games, order and quietness. After schooling, she was a diligent worker at the Jefferson County workshop, saving $2500 in cash in her suitcase, which she kept under her bed. She enjoyed her own apartment with her friends and counselor, but came home every weekend. After surgery from a fall, she passed away quietly at 57, following an evening party with family and friends, eating Kentucky fried chicken and singing camp songs together. Jesus was her "very best friend."

Ruth, with brown hair and eyes, was quiet like her dad. After her first dance and date with Ricky Roberts, she declared, as she twirled around in her new yellow dress, that she wanted to be a teenager forever. She pursued a nursing career, and later married Ray, an environmental engineer, and moved to Idaho.

Marty, another curly redhead, with a mind of her own, was a challenge. If she wanted to do something, she did it, regardless of the circumstances. If she was disciplined, she'd reply, "That's okay, it was worth it!" She wanted to be a teacher, received her degree, married Mike, an engineer from the Colorado School of Mines, and moved to New Mexico to begin her family with their daughter Melissa. She is now a teacher-librarian at Standley Lake High School in Jefferson County.

2
My Last Teaching Assignment

It was a balmy, snowy day in the 1980s. The snowflakes reluctantly fell to the ground and melted. The phone rang as I hurried down the steps. It was the Jefferson County substitute office. The voice was appealing.

"I know, Mrs. Ogle, that you decided not to teach anymore since your husband 's stroke, but there's no one else—Christmas holidays coming up, you know. It's only an afternoon assignment." She sounded very tired as she continued," It's junior high English, the teacher got very sick and...."

"No problem," I quickly replied, "Jack takes his nap in the afternoon."

She relayed the details and I put down the phone. Junior high! On a Friday afternoon! My forte in Jefferson County had been third grade. I smiled, though, as I thought of teaching all eight grades in the Colorado mountains and on the Wyoming prairie. Eighth graders can be very challenging, especially on a Friday afternoon!

Jack raised his head from his bed and asked, "Who was on the phone?!" Straightening his blanket, I assured him I'd be home by a little after three and that this really would be my last teaching assignment. I pondered the word "last".... After 30 years of teaching, 27 in Jefferson County, would it really be my last?

The school was on 88th Ave., just a block west of Wadsworth. The kids were streaming out of the building, then retreating in from the cold and fluttering snowflakes. I reported to the office and made my way through the maze of students to the assigned room. The lesson plans had been scrawled hastily and laid on the desk, "Here are the words for the spelling test, and then they can read quietly."

Read quietly! It's Friday! Thanks much!

Very quickly the bell rang and the troops filtered in, many still with their leftover lunches.

One boy exclaimed, "Oh, a sub today!" Squeals of fun and laughter ran through the group.

Oh, I thought, this is great! A spelling test and read quietly!

We got through the spelling test. I collected the papers as the noise level began to rise. I said, "You know, nothing much is planned. I have a poem from *As You Like It*, by Shakespeare, but perhaps it would be too hard. It's really senior high-level."

"Oh no," piped up one boy, "we can do it!"

"Yeah ! Yeah!" Others joined in.

"Okay, we'll try it!" I replied.

I passed out drawing paper and they divided it into squares as I read the first four lines of the poem

.

All the world's a stage,
And all the men and women merely players;
They have their exits and their entrances,
And one man in his time plays many parts.

"So what was your first role in life?" I asked.

"Being born!"

"Right, in the first square draw yourself as a ba-by while I read Shakespeare's description of the ba-by.... 'At first, the infant, mewling and puking in the nurse's arms.' Then what?"

With a groan! "School, school and more school!"

Shakespeare's words on the school years, "then the whining schoolboy, with his satchel and shining morning face, creeping like a snail unwillingly to school."

On we went through Shakespeare's stages—the lover, the soldier, the justice and then the "old man." As I read the last eight lines describing the old man with his loose fitting pants, spectacles on his nose, shrunken age, losing his voice, teeth, sight and taste, expressions came from the class.

"Oh yeah, that's my grandpa!"

They finished their sketches, telling each other their dreams. The bell rang and as they were leaving, one boy turned back to say, "See ya, Mrs. Ogle."

"Sure, no problem!"

3
Jack

When Jack had his massive stroke in 1987, our lives changed. What followed were more than 17 years together at home. His speech returned, he began slowly to walk; his left side was completely paralyzed. There were good days and not-so-good days. Jack said we could have one cranky day a week, but not on the same day! Also included in the package was one cry day. For me that was usually when the silence of the night and the weariness of my body crept into my life. But the Psalms tell us, "Weeping endures but for a night but joy comes in the morning!" and the cloud began to lift. We read books together, Viktor Frankl's *Man's Search for Meaning* being one of our favorites. Jack would enjoy the letters from our friends in faraway places and their visits when they came home for a spell. Jack would say, "Get out the wheels, Honey," in reference to his wheelchair, and off we'd go...to the mountains, picnic on the lake at Georgetown with friends, and Elderhostels, leaving cold, snowy Colorado for spring in Arizona. When someone inquired about his health, he'd reply, "Half a body is better than none." His evening prayer included the phrase, "Thank you, Lord, for the measure of health you have given us." This was his legacy.

Each evening, before he rode the chair lift upstairs, he'd stop at the organ to play his favorite hymn by Stuart Hamblen.

> But until then my heart will go on singing,
> Until then with joy I'll carry on,
> Until the day my eyes behold the city,
> Until the day God calls me home.

On the day before God called him home, we all celebrated his 78th birthday upstairs in his room. Later that day, he came down, dressed in his white shirt and Levi's, and announced, "I'm going out on the scooter."

"Well, okay," I said hesitantly and reluctantly, "I'll get my sweater."

"No, I'm going with Michael." Michael was our youngest grandson and Jack's fishing partner. (When

Jack had his second stroke, Ruth and her husband Ray moved back to Colorado. Marty and Mike had moved home earlier with Melissa and Maria. They later had two boys, Morgan and Michael.) When Jack and Michael turned the corner, out of my eyesight, Jack turned up the speed as Michael ran along.

The next morning he quietly slipped home as I lay by his side. His body was laid in the old Arvada Cemetery, which he laughingly called "our last piece of real estate." Friends and family lingered in our backyard that day "just remembering," until the moon and stars came out to join us.

4
Returning to Ulm

I went to Ulm today with my daughter Ruth and her husband Ray. I wanted to see the small town and the schoolhouse that had been my home during my first teaching assignment many years ago.

We had stopped at the library research room in Sheridan and read how Ulm had flourished during the Homestead Act. Large ranches were accumulated. The town boasted a lumber company, a community hall, mercantile store, post office and a two-room schoolhouse. It had been a robust, busy gathering place for the thriving families. Then World War I, the Depression and World War II crowded in to change their lives forever.

When I taught there 66 years ago, there was one small post office with a few supplies, the Grange, one farmhouse and the schoolhouse. Today, I would see remnants of that small isolated spot on the windswept prairie. We left Sheridan in the late afternoon. The highway was like a ribbon stretching endlessly over the green rolling hills. Then the Ulm turn-off appeared. The road was not paved, but was narrow with rocky ground. The ranchers called those "washboard" roads. We bumped along endlessly as it followed the railroad tracks, which held endless cars heaped with coal from the mines. We saw a sign for "East Ulm" and then caught sight of a clump of trees hiding some old buildings.

"I think we missed it."

"Well, we'll just turn around and see."

We turned around and stopped. A very old farmhouse was valiantly holding up a caving roof as it sloped toward the ground. A broken gate, a tattered fence, a weathered barn and outbuildings were scattered in disarray. I had walked to that farmhouse from the schoolhouse to get two buckets of water each day. Jimmy and Bob had walked though that gate and sauntered up to the school each morning and again at lunch time. We were unable to enter their yard, so we drove up to the schoolhouse.

There it was! The shady trees seemed to be protecting the old school building as they bent over it with their scraggly limbs. We squeezed though the metal gate, which had a rusty padlock linked to an old chain.

The knee-high wheat grass was everywhere, swaying in the warm summer wind. We tramped through the grass as we reverently approached the school. The tan siding was peeling, revealing the original white painted boards.

I had to come back, old friend, one more time—just to remember.

The porch and steps were gone. It had been such a favorite place, talking and eating our lunches on the steps with our lard lunch pails, greeting a new day, and sitting on the steps at the close of the day as the stars slowly came out.

We walked up the planks to the door and gave the reluctant door a heavy push. Numerous bugs began scurrying about. Dust and dirt swirled around our feet. I opened the door to my old room—no bed, no stove, no coal bucket—not anything but the familiar faded green wainscoting encircling the small room. I closed the door, anxious to see the classroom.

The door creaked as I opened it. The silence of the classroom was overwhelming. The late afternoon sun was streaming through the dusty windows, landing on the empty broken desks. The stove and teacher's desk were gone, no books or cupboard in the corner, and the cracked blackboards had been visited with a Dick and Jane story barely visible plus greetings from returning students over the years. The gunny-sack bulletin board had two charts, one "Alaska," the other "Good Food,"—both with pasted, curled magazine pictures. I paused for a minute. I could hear the children laughing, and playing in the school yard. We walked out slowly and quietly.

We walked through the waving wheat grass. I looked up to see Watermelon Hill. In the fall, we'd tramp up with our lunches. Hedwik's boys, Jimmy and Bob, would bring up a bushel basketful of juicy round watermelons. The boys would crack them open on the rocks and we'd all relish the cool, juicy melons. Then we'd roll the leftover rinds down the hill.

"C'mon, Mom," called Ruth from the car. "We'd better get going."

It was a quiet ride home.

5
Ending Thoughts

I leave this memoir with you, knowing that at 88 my life is fading, even as the morning sunrise fades away. The spring flowers are in bloom. Soon the summer flowers will take their place. The butterflies fly away in their luster, while the worms cultivate our earth—each in their place and in their time. Each person is precious, and has a place, and the choice to bloom where they are planted.

I found a new verse in the Good Book recently, "Even when a man is 'very old,' let him rejoice every day of his life!" I wonder if 88 is "very old?"

6
Poetry

I learned to love poetry from my mother, who read to us after supper each evening. Later in life, when I was the poetry consultant in Jefferson County, Colorado, I compiled "Poems to Live by and to Enjoy...A Compilation of Favorites for the Classroom." These were classic poems that emphasized the key values of life.

One of my favorites was a 1903 poem by Edmund Cooke. This poem, "Trouble," proved to be most helpful, as many of our children have and will experience real trouble in their young lives—divorce, separation, rejection, etc. We *all* learned the first verse of the poem. We clapped to it, marched to it, and recited it often, and it became my trademark in many situations.

I wrote "To Those Who Work with the Handicapped..." in reference to my handicapped daughter, Beth. "Love Is...," which was published in the *Denver Post*, is my philosophy of teaching.

Trouble

Did you tackle that trouble that came your way
With a resolute heart and cheerful?
Or hide your face from the light of day
With a craven soul and fearful?
Oh, a trouble's a ton, or a trouble's an ounce
Or a trouble is what you make it,
It isn't the fact that you're hurt that counts
But only how did you take it?

To those who work with the handicapped…

We are the parents.
Before our child was born,
We did not choose
A handicapped child.

But you,
You, who work daily with handicapped children,
You, with your brains, your education,
And physical capabilities,
You chose to work with our children,
You chose to give a large part of your day,
Of your life, of your thoughts, of your self
To these, our children,
Who need so much help.

You chose to do this.
For this, we are thankful.
We depend on you,
We appreciate you,
And we love you,
Because you made that decision.

The Parents

LOVE is...

Though I use all the latest educational terms and methods of men and of educators and have not love for each child in my classroom, I am become as sounding brass, or a tinkling cymbal.

And though I have the gift of public relations and understand the parents, telling them what they want to hear...but have not love for my children, I am nothing.

And though I buy books and games for my classroom, and though I stay late each evening and have not love for each child... it profiteth me nothing.

Love is very patient and kind with each little one, love enjoys to teach, to see their eyes glisten, to hear them read with pride in their voices...

Love does not feel a need to impress either parents or supervisors...seeketh not its own. Love is not easily provoked or irritated with each little ones' "Oh teacher..." or the noise and confusion of little ones' learning.

Love is having a silent hush at story time, love is children crowding around your desk, love is playing together outside, love is show & tell time. **Love is teaching children.**